BELIEVE

MEETING JESUS IN THE SCRIPTURES

A Catholic Guide for Small Groups

the
evangelical
catholic

forming disciples.
training leaders.

and

theWORD
among us®
press

Published by The Word Among Us Press
7115 Guilford Drive, Suite 100
Frederick, Maryland 21704
www.wau.org

20 19 18 17 16   2 3 4 5 6

Nihil obstat: The Reverend Michael Morgan, J.D., J.C.L.
                   Censor Librorum
                   May 27, 2015

Imprimatur: Most Reverend Felipe J. Estevez
                   Bishop of St. Augustine
                   May 27, 2015

ISBN: 978-1-59325-281-6
eISBN: 978-1-59325-474-2

Cover design by Andrea Alvarez

Made and printed in the United States of America

Library of Congress Control Number: 2015944821

Contents

Introduction

"If you would **believe,** you would see
the glory of God."

John 11:40

What does it mean to believe?

At different times in life, the big questions force themselves on us. "Where am I going?" "What am I looking for in life?" "Why am I here?"

These questions caught up with me in high school when my parents divorced. It took me by surprise. I had trusted in my parents' marriage, *depended* on it. My life was created and held in that reality.

When my parents split, I realized an important fact: they were broken, imperfect people. Ultimately, my faith in their marriage was unfounded. I asked myself, "What *can* I believe in?"

Sometimes difficulties bring clarity that is impossible when times are good. In this new light on my life, I scrutinized many things I had previously taken for granted. I asked fundamental questions. Is God to be trusted? Is Jesus someone I can rely on? Can I put my faith in him?

When Christians talk about "faith," the word is often used ambiguously. Consider these phrases:

- "I was raised in the faith."
- "She is strong in her faith."
- "I would like to learn more about my faith."

In these expressions, "faith" is a stand-alone noun. You might get the sense that "my faith" or "the faith" is a collection of teachings, rules, or doctrines to be studied. But these are shorthand uses for the word "faith." For Christians, "faith" sums up a whole reality: we believe in *someone*. Try completing the sentences with "faith in Jesus" instead of just "faith." Does it add another level of meaning for you?

We often learn about faith through good, healthy relationships, when we have people in our lives we can trust and count on, who will come through for us and stand by us in tough times. They teach us how to have faith in others and not only in ourselves.

We can have that same kind of faith in Jesus, if we come to know him and trust him. Even though at times people will disappoint or even betray us, Christians experience Jesus and know he is different. He is worthy of absolute trust: faith in Jesus never disappoints us.

You don't have to take my word for it. This small group guide that you have in your hand will introduce you to the person of Jesus. It's impossible to know, trust, or believe in any person unless you first get to know that person. What is important to him? What does she care about? Who does he hang out with?

People who wanted to find the answers to those questions two thousand years ago sought out Jesus. Their encounters with him changed their lives, sometimes beyond recognition. Jesus' followers wrote down stories of these experiences with Jesus so that they could be shared far and wide and preserved forever.

Each week you will have the chance to read one of these stories and, if you are part of a small group, to discuss it with others.

You will be able to decide for yourself whether Jesus is worthy of trust. Do his teachings seem true or false, inspired or delusional, full of life and hope or laughable?

Learn what he says, see how he reacts, and evaluate how he responds to people's questions, fears, and concerns. Then consider: "What, if anything, does Jesus mean, or could he mean, for my life?"

A small group is a great place to start looking for answers with other people who are also seeking what to believe, or who already know but want to be with others seeking and asking important questions. While talking, laughing, and praying together, you will meet Jesus through small group members who already trust Jesus. If they're committed followers, they will show you something of what he is like.

The "Encountering Christ This Week" exercises in each session will help you meet Jesus through prayer. It's difficult to put faith in Jesus if he seems very removed from your life. But Jesus told his followers, "Where two or three are gathered in my name, there am I in the midst of them" (Matthew 18:20) and "I am with you always, to the close of the age" (28:20). The small group and weekly prayer and Scripture exercises will help you figure out if this is true or not.

"Ask, and it will be given you; seek, and you will find; knock, and it will be opened to you. For every one who asks receives, and he who seeks finds, and to him who knocks it will be opened" (Luke 11:9-10).

Jesus said that. Christians believe he wants us to be honest and straightforward with him about our lives, our needs, our hopes and dreams.

The journey is your own to make. Take the risk. Commit to the small group, or to praying through this book on your own.

Find out for yourself what it means to believe.

Andrea Lauren Jackson
Pastoral Associate, St. Julia Parish of Weston and Lincoln, Massachusetts, and former Evangelical Catholic missionary

How to Use This Small Group Guide

Welcome to *Believe*, a small group guide to help people meet Jesus of Nazareth and know him more deeply.

Weekly Sessions

The crux of this small group guide is the weekly session materials themselves. Here you will find opening and closing prayer suggestions, the Scripture passages to be discussed that week, questions for discussion, ideas for action, and prayer prompts to carry you through the week.

Unlike some small group Scripture discussion guides that progress consecutively through a book of the Bible, each session in this guide is self-contained. That way, if you or a friend attends for the first time on Week 3, there won't be a need to "catch up"; anyone can just dive right in with the rest of the group. Instead of building sequentially, the sessions deepen thematically, helping you engage more with Jesus little by little.

The more you take notes, jot down ideas or questions, underline verses in your Bible (if you bring one to your small group), and refer back to previous sessions, the more God has the opportunity to speak to you through the discussion and the ideas he has placed in your heart. As with anything else, the more you put in, the more you get back.

The best way to take advantage of each week's discussion is to carry the theme into your life by using the "Encountering Christ This Week" section. Think of this as a launching pad to meet Jesus every day. Your small group facilitator will talk about the recommendations during each session. You will have a chance to ask questions and share experiences from previous weeks.

If you're not in a small group, *Believe* can be used on your own by considering the questions asked of each Scripture passage and following up with the suggestions in "Encountering Christ This Week."

Appendices

Helpful appendices for both participants and facilitators supplement the weekly materials. Appendices A through D are for participants, and Appendices E through G are for group facilitators.

Prior to your first group meeting, please read Appendix A, "Small Group Discussion Guide." These guidelines will help every person in the group set a respectful tone that creates the space for encountering Christ.

This small group will differ from other discussion groups you may have experienced. Is it a lecture? No. A book club? No. Appendix A will help you understand what this small group is and how you can help seek a "Spirit-led" discussion. Every member is responsible for the quality of the group dynamics. This appendix will give you helpful tidbits for being a supportive and involved member of the group.

Appendices B, C, and D provide resources to enhance and deepen your relationship with Jesus. In Appendix B, you will find a step-by-step guide for reading Scripture on your own. It will show you how to meditate and apply what you find there. Appendix D suggests Scripture passages that are rich in content and have been used by many for encountering Christ. Choose a passage linked to a topic that draws your attention, or just use the Internet to search "Scripture passage on _____."

Appendix B also offers help in finding other spiritual reading that can enhance and deepen your appreciation for the teachings and person of Jesus.

In Appendix C, you will find a guide to the Sacrament of Reconciliation. Commonly known as "Confession," the Sacrament of Reconciliation bridges the distance between us and God that can be caused by a variety of reasons, including unrepented sin. If you want to grow closer to Jesus and experience great peace, the Sacrament of Reconciliation is an indispensable way to close the gap. This appendix leads you through the steps of preparing for and going to Confession in order to lessen the anxiety that you might feel.

While Appendices A–D are important for participants and facilitators alike, Appendices E–G support the facilitator in his or her role.

A facilitator is not a teacher. His or her role is to support and encourage fruitful group discussion and tend to the group dynamics.

In Appendix E, the group facilitator will find guidance and best practices for facilitating a small group successfully. We've put together recommendations for some possible pesky group dynamics. You will find guidelines on what makes a great group work: building genuine friendships, calling for the Holy Spirit to be the group's true facilitator, and seeking joy together.

Appendix F takes the facilitator from the general to the specific, providing detailed leader notes for each session in *Believe*. Use this appendix as you prepare for each week's group meeting. The notes give you a "head's up" on some of the content or context of the Scripture passage to be discussed that might be confusing or sufficiently important that the facilitator should draw attention to it. The notes also give tips for how to build group dynamics from week to week.

Appendix G helps the facilitator in leading prayer and encouraging participation in prayer by group members. While the material in each session includes a suggested prayer, Appendix G guides the facilitator in how to pray aloud extemporaneously and help others in the group to do so as well.

Learning this skill is important. It will model for the group members how to talk to Jesus in their own words. Closing with extemporaneous prayers is an extremely valuable way to honor the time you have spent together by offering up the discoveries, questions, and joys of your conversation. Appendix G will help you guide your group from awkward beginnings to a deepening experience of talking to God.

Appendix G also gives the facilitator more information about how to use the "Encounter Christ This Week" section of each week's materials. You should encourage and support the group's members in their personal engagement with the week's topic through their deepening commitment to allowing Jesus to become more and more a part of their lives.

Enjoy the adventure!

He sought to see
who Jesus was ...

haeus

so he ran on ahead
and climbed up into
a sycamore tree.

Luke 19:3-4

Read aloud the following passage from **Psalm 37** and then ask someone to pray aloud the prayer that follows.

All | In the name of the Father, and of the Son, and of the Holy Spirit. **Amen.**

Leader

Trust in the LORD, and do good;
    so you will dwell in the land, and
        enjoy security.
Take delight in the LORD,
    and he will give you the desires of
        your heart.
Commit your way to the LORD;
    trust in him, and he will act.

Psalm 37:3-5

Reader

God, teach us to enjoy you and to be open to you. Guide our discussion through your Holy Spirit. Help us seek you together. Direct our conversation that we may know who you are. Thank you for being with us.

All We pray this in the name of the Father, and of the Son, and of the Holy Spirit. **Amen.**

What are your
current thoughts
or feelings
about Jesus?

Luke

[1]He entered Jericho and was passing through. [2]And there was a man named Zacchaeus; he was a chief tax collector, and rich. [3]And he sought to see who Jesus was, but could not, on account of the crowd, because he was small of stature. [4]So he ran on ahead and climbed up into a sycamore tree to see him, for he was to pass that way. [5]And when Jesus came to the place, he looked up and said to him, "Zacchaeus,

19:1-10

make haste and come down; for I must stay at your house today." [6]So he made haste and came down, and received him joyfully. [7]And when they saw it they all murmured, "He has gone in to be the guest of a man who is a sinner." [8]And Zacchaeus stood and said to the Lord, "Behold, Lord, the half of my goods I give to the poor; and if I have defrauded any one of anything, I restore it fourfold." [9]And Jesus said to him, "Today salvation has come to this house, since he also is a son of Abraham. [10]For the Son of man came to seek and to save the lost."

1. Who are the main players in this narrative? What role does each play?

2. What does Zacchaeus do in order to see Jesus? What does this tell you about Zacchaeus?

3. Jews considered tax collectors thieves and ruffians who collaborated with the Roman Empire, the detested foreign and pagan military occupier of Israel. How does this information influence your understanding of Zacchaeus climbing the tree to see Jesus?

4. Why do you think Jesus singled out Zacchaeus?

5. Does anything strike you about what Jesus says to Zacchaeus?

6. How does Zacchaeus respond to Jesus' request to stay at his house? What does he do and say? What does this reveal about Zacchaeus?

7. Does Jesus seem pleased with Zacchaeus? Why do you think Jesus pronounces salvation before Zacchaeus follows through?

8. How do you think Zacchaeus might have felt after Jesus spoke to him (verses 9-10)? Have you ever experienced Jesus' kindness and mercy in such a way? What was that like?

9. How is Zacchaeus' approach to learning about Jesus similar to your own? How is it different?

10. What are some ways you can "climb the sycamore tree" and seek Jesus more in your life?

Revelation 3:20

Behold, I stand at the door and knock; if anyone hears my voice and opens the door, I will come in to him and eat with him, and he with me.

We seek something more than the material world because God is seeking us, knocking on our door. Christians believe God created humans with hearts that instinctively need God precisely to inspire us to answer the door! The God who is love made us to know and love him:

> I will give them a heart to know that I am the LORD;
> and they shall be my people and I will be their God,
> for they shall return to me with their whole heart.
> (Jeremiah 24:7)

When we seek Jesus, things happen—often unexpected things, as Zacchaeus learned. He wanted just to see Jesus, but then he found Jesus inviting himself to dinner!

This week, plan a time and place to seek Jesus. Try setting aside five to ten minutes each day. It doesn't matter whether you sit, stand, or walk—just talk to him. At some point, do as Zacchaeus did in verse 8: share with Jesus who you are and what you hope to become in the future. You can write this out as a letter to Jesus or you can speak the words aloud. Though at first this may feel awkward, it can be a very useful tool for keeping you focused and open. Jesus always listens attentively. Try to trust that he is present to you even if you don't feel him.

Allow quiet time for Jesus to respond. Sometimes you will sense him speaking back to you. Other times God is more elusive. He may speak very subtly at times, placing a thought in our minds or bringing something to our memories or imagination.

In this way, he respects our human freedom. God will not overwhelm us with his presence. That would make a free choice to know and love him impossible. It's up to us to trust that Jesus is knocking and then engage the thoughts or memories that arise when you are with him.

Climb the sycamore!

All | In the name of
the Father, and
of the Son, and of
the Holy Spirit.
Amen.

Reader | Jesus,
We praise you for the example of Zacchaeus.
Thank you for your presence in our discussion.
Please help make the inspirations you have stirred within us a reality in our hearts and lives.
Help us to be willing to seek you with sincere hearts, and to open wide the doors of our hearts to you.
We pray this through Christ our Lord.

All | **Amen.**

week**2**

blind

Barti

Take heart maeus rise, he is calling you.

Mark 10:49

Have one person read the prayer aloud while the others pray along silently.

All | In the name of the Father, and of the Son, and of the Holy Spirit. **Amen.**

Reader

Father,
We praise you for the love and compassion you have for us.

Thank you for gathering us together to reflect on your word.

Holy Spirit, enlighten our minds and open our hearts so that we may learn how to more closely follow Jesus.

Please inspire and guide our discussion.

We pray this through Christ our Lord.

All | **Amen.**

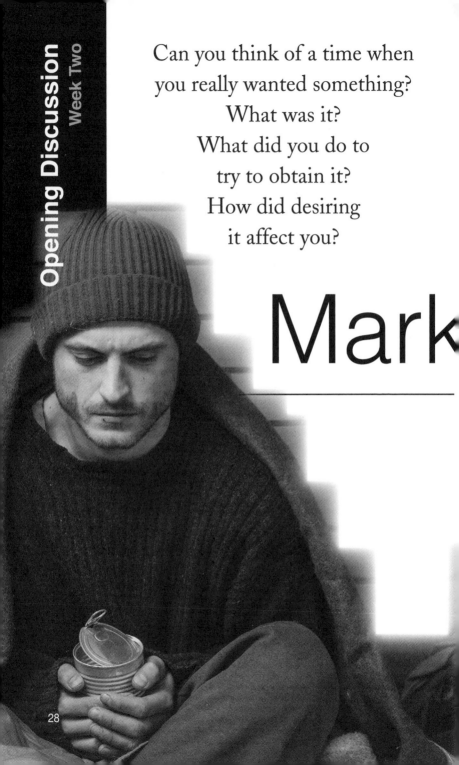

Can you think of a time when
you really wanted something?
What was it?
What did you do to
try to obtain it?
How did desiring
it affect you?

Mark

⁴⁶And they came to Jericho; and as he was leaving Jericho with his disciples and a great multitude, Bartimaeus, a blind beggar, the son of Timaeus, was sitting by the roadside. ⁴⁷And when he heard that it was Jesus of Nazareth, he began to cry out and say, "Jesus, Son of David, have mercy on me!" ⁴⁸And many rebuked him, telling him to be silent; but he cried out all the more, "Son of David, have

10:46-52

mercy on me!" ⁴⁹And Jesus stopped and said, "Call him." And they called the blind man, saying to him, "Take heart; rise, he is calling you." ⁵⁰And throwing off his mantle he sprang up and came to Jesus. ⁵¹And Jesus said to him, "What do you want me to do for you?" And the blind man said to him, "Master, let me receive my sight." ⁵²And Jesus said to him, "Go your way; your faith has made you well." And immediately he received his sight and followed him on the way.

1. Describe the scene. Who is passing by? Who is sitting at the roadside? What do you think the atmosphere is like?

2. What does Bartimaeus do when he hears that it is Jesus of Nazareth passing by?

3. How does the crowd respond to Bartimaeus' cries for help? Why might the people have reacted this way?

4. How do you think Bartimaeus felt when the crowd "rebuked" him (verse 48)?

5. Are discouragement and disapproval from others obstacles for you to getting closer to Jesus? How so?

6. What might Bartimaeus' mantle symbolize (verse 50)?

7. Read verse 51. If Jesus asked you this question, what would you say?

8. Bartimaeus had great faith. What might have inspired his strong faith? What is your response to the gift of faith that God extends to each of us? What gets in your way of trying to believe in Jesus?

9. How might the Holy Spirit be leading you to respond to Jesus passing by? How is the Holy Spirit stirring you to grow in your faith in Jesus?

All people have needs: tangible needs, such as food, water, and oxygen, as well as intangible needs for love, forgiveness, friendship, and family. We and our loved ones, like Bartimaeus, also have needs for health and well-being. Even strong desires often feel like needs: vacations when we're weary, a better car that doesn't break down, or a faster smart phone.

Are you in the habit of asking God for what you need? Many people do, and many people feel disappointed because it seems that their prayers were not answered.

People who pray regularly experience peace and hope no matter what the outcome of their requests. They trust that God is working, either in obvious or subtle ways.

Most who experience this peace spend their time with God asking for what they need. But they also spend time praying in other ways—by praising God, repenting of any sin, and thanking him.

An easy way to balance your conversation with God is to use the acronym **ACTS: Adoration, Contrition, Thanksgiving, and Supplication.** Decide how much time you will spend in prayer.

Twenty minutes a day is ideal, but pray how you can, not at a time or in a way you can't. Divide your prayer time between these four ways of praying:

Adoration: This sometimes feels awkward at first. Start with the basics: try admiring or praising God for the beauty of creation or the people in your life. God made them all! Or prayerfully read one of these praise psalms from your Bible every day: Psalms 19, 33, 92, 103, 138, 146, 147, 148.

Contrition: Look inside yourself to see if anything in your life sits uneasily. Ask Jesus if something is getting in the way of your relationship with him. Explore the question with Jesus. To remove any obstacles, pray the words of Bartimaeus: "Jesus, have mercy on me!"

Thanksgiving: Make this very specific: recent events that made you happy, physical gifts you received, an unexpected kindness when you desperately needed it, a much-desired day off from study or work, the recovery of a loved one.

Supplication: Ask God for everything you need. Ask on behalf of your loved ones as well. Request God to open your eyes to see how he is responding. Tell him you need his help to see some of the ways he is working in your life.

Finally, spend a minute or two in silence, resting in God. Try this at least twice before the next meeting so that you can share with the group how it went for you.

Let us then with confidence draw near to the throne of grace, that we may receive mercy and find grace to help in time of need
(Hebrews 4:16)

Ask someone to read the following prayer, attributed to **St. Augustine of Hippo**.

All | In the name of the Father, and of the Son, and of the Holy Spirit. **Amen.**

Reader | O Lord my God,
I believe in you,
Father, Son, and Holy Spirit. . . .
Insofar as I can,
insofar as you have given me the power,
I have sought you.
I became weary and I labored.
O Lord my God,
my sole hope,
help me to believe
and never to cease seeking you.
Grant that I may always and ardently
seek your face.
Give me the strength to seek you,
for you help me to find you,
and you have more and more given me
the hope of finding you.
Here I am before you. . . .
Enable me to remember you,
to understand you,
and to love you.

All | **Amen.**

week**3**

Jesus Teaches about

Fear not, little flock, for it is your Father's good pleasure to **Worry** and Fear give you the kingdom."

Luke 12:32

Ask one person to read the following prayer.

All | In the name of the Father, and of the Son, and of the Holy Spirit. **Amen.**

Reader | Lord, we invite you into this place.
Please be present with us.
Help us to be honest with our-
selves and each other as we talk
and pray.
Help us to understand how our
worries and fears distract us from
experiencing true joy.
Help us to put our trust in you.
We pray this through Christ our
Lord.

All | **Amen.**

What do you worry
about most often?

Luke

²²And [Jesus] said to his disciples, "Therefore I tell you, do not be anxious about your life, what you shall eat, nor about your body, what you shall put on. ²³For life is more than food, and the body more than clothing. ²⁴Consider the ravens: they neither sow nor reap, they have neither storehouse nor barn, and yet God feeds them. Of how much more value are you than the birds! ²⁵And which of you by being anxious can add a cubit to his span of life? ²⁶If then you are not able to do as small a thing as that, why are you anxious about the rest? ²⁷Consider the lilies, how they grow; they neither toil nor spin; yet I tell you,

2:22-34

even Solomon in all his glory was not arrayed like one of these. ²⁸But if God so clothes the grass which is alive in the field today and tomorrow is thrown into the oven, how much more will he clothe you, O men of little faith! ²⁹And do not seek what you are to eat and what you are to drink, nor be of anxious mind. ³⁰For all the nations of the world seek these things; and your Father knows that you need them. ³¹Instead, seek his kingdom, and these things shall be yours as well.

³²"Fear not, little flock, for it is your Father's good pleasure to give you the kingdom. ³³Sell your possessions, and give alms; provide yourselves with purses that do not grow old, with a treasure in the heavens that does not fail, where no thief approaches and no moth destroys. ³⁴For where your treasure is, there will your heart be also."

1. What do you think motivates Jesus to give such a long teaching on not worrying?

2. Jesus gives several reasons not to worry. How many can you identify? Which one is most meaningful to you?

3. How would you describe an "anxious mind" (verse 29)?

4. What does Jesus tell his disciples they should be seeking? What do you think this might mean?

5. What do you think it means for the Father to give the disciples the kingdom?

6. What most tempts you to worry? Given that, what do you learn about yourself?

7. Do you know anyone who has mastered worry and sought the Father's kingdom before everything else? What is that person's faith like?

8. Find the verbs in this passage that relate to God the Father's actions (verses 24, 28, 30, and 32). Given these, what do you think Jesus is communicating about the Father's character?

9. Which aspect of God's character stands out to you? Does this speak to the area(s) where you tend towards worry or lack of trust? How?

10. What are some practical things that have helped you overcome worry and replace it with God's peace?

11. How might the Holy Spirit be calling you to trust him more?

The range of what causes us to worry and feel anxious is broad and varied. Jesus encourages us to seek only his kingdom, depending on the Father for all that we need.

Sometimes it seems as if God doesn't want to meet our needs. Some situations remain intractable: perhaps we lose our job and can't find another, or maybe our future career is on the line because we can't seem to master a discipline we need.

When these situations or other difficulties arise and persist, we wonder why God doesn't hear our prayer and *help* us. What else *can* we do but be plagued by worry?

Trust God—that's what we can do, if we learn to grow to trust Jesus. St. Paul wrote to the Romans, "We know that in everything God works for good with those who love him" (8:28). If we believe this is true, then we think about everything in life differently. It becomes possible to grow in faith and dependence on God, no matter what our circumstances.

St. Paul said to the Philippians:

> Have no anxiety about anything, but in everything by prayer and supplication with thanksgiving let your requests be made known to God. And the peace of God, which passes all understanding, will keep your hearts and your minds in Christ Jesus. (4:6-7)

If you have particular worries and fears, make them known to God, just as St. Paul exhorted the Philippians to do. Share your anxieties with Jesus as you would share with a best friend or with a perfect parent who knows you fully, accepts you unconditionally, and loves you just the way you need to be loved.

Allow yourself to be with God honestly and freely. God knows you better than anyone else. Neither our failings nor our successes influence his love and care.

If it helps you focus, write out your worries and fears in a journal as a way to share them with Jesus. Then trust him for the peace he promises us: "And the peace of God, which passes all understanding, will keep your hearts and your minds in Christ Jesus" (Philippians 4:7).

Try praying the simple prayer "Jesus, I trust you." Even if your feelings are far from this, pray it as an act of faith. As you exercise faith, God will come and do what he promises—give you peace.

Be bold in your prayer and thank him in advance for the peace you know he gives. Spend as much time as you wish with God, but aim for at least fifteen to twenty minutes. People who pray regularly attest that it takes twenty minutes to quiet the mind, allowing time for God to come into their hearts.

If you are Catholic, be intentional about confessing the sin of worry when you go to the Sacrament of Reconciliation. When you confess, be specific about what worries you. Tell the Lord you are sorry for your lack of faith.

Jesus wants us to have greater freedom and joy. He will work this freedom in us as we open ourselves to him through prayer and the sacraments.

During the week, try to focus on letting God provide for you by praying this simple prayer: "Jesus, I trust you." Simply repeat it a few times when you feel fear or worry overtaking your thoughts. If worry and anxiety are burdens for you, memorize Romans 8:28 so that you have it available whenever you need it.

After all who wish have had a chance to pray extemporaneously, ask one person to close the prayer.

All | In the name of the Father, and of the Son, and of the Holy Spirit. **Amen.**

Reader | Dear Lord,
Every day my fears make me worry
about the future.
I believe it all rests on me.
You say to become like a little child
and put my trust in you.
I can't do that without your help, God.
My heart has little trust and harbors
many fears.
Help me to believe that you can change
these things in me, Lord.
Help me to grow in trust.
Help me to know that I am your child.
Jesus, I put my trust in you.

All | **Amen.**

Healing

"Do you want

at the **Pool**

to be healed?" John 5:6

Ask someone to read the following prayer aloud.

All | In the name of the Father, and of the Son, and of the Holy Spirit. **Amen.**

Reader God, we know that you
are here.
We know that you see us
and you hear us.
We know that you seek to heal
us and make us whole.
Help us to hear your voice,
both now together and in our
own prayers.
We ask this in Jesus' name.

All Amen.

What do you think about miracles? Do you believe that they still happen today? Or that they happened in Jesus' time but not now? Or neither?

John

¹After this there was a feast of the Jews, and Jesus went up to Jerusalem.

²Now there is in Jerusalem by the Sheep Gate a pool, in Hebrew called Beth-za'tha, which has five porticoes. ³In these lay a multitude of invalids, blind, lame, paralyzed. ⁵One man was there, who had been ill for thirty-eight years. ⁶When Jesus saw him and knew that he had been lying there a long time, he said to him, "Do you want to be healed?" ⁷The sick man answered him, "Sir, I have no man to put me into the pool when the water is troubled, and while I am going another steps down before me." ⁸Jesus said to

5:1-15

him, "Rise, take up your pallet, and walk." ⁹And at once the man was healed, and he took up his pallet and walked.

Now that day was the sabbath. ¹⁰So the Jews said to the man who was cured, "It is the sabbath, it is not lawful for you to carry your pallet." ¹¹But he answered them, "The man who healed me said to me, 'Take up your pallet, and walk.'" ¹²They asked him, "Who is the man who said to you, 'Take up your pallet, and walk'?" ¹³Now the man who had been healed did not know who it was, for Jesus had withdrawn, as there was a crowd in the place. ¹⁴Afterward, Jesus found him in the temple, and said to him, "See, you are well! Sin no more, that nothing worse befall you." ¹⁵The man went away and told the Jews that it was Jesus who had healed him.

1. How long had the man in the story been sick?

2. Can you tell what his condition seemed to be in comparison with the other sick people at the pool?

3. Why do you think Jesus might have chosen this sick man over the others?

4. The sick man speaks twice in this passage (verses 7 and 11). What can you tell about his character from what he says?

5. Where does Jesus find the man after he is healed? What does this tell you about the man?

6. Do you think Jesus was looking for the man? What might have motivated Jesus to look for him?

7. Read verse 14. What facial expression or emotion do you picture Jesus having as he speaks to the man?

8. What can we learn about Jesus through this story?

9. What does Jesus seem to need in us for him to have a relationship with us?

All of us have struggles: personal, relational, professional. Sometimes these struggles involve physical diseases, sometimes other impediments. We become "stuck" in many different ways, thinking that we can't make our bodies, our jobs, or our relationships right.

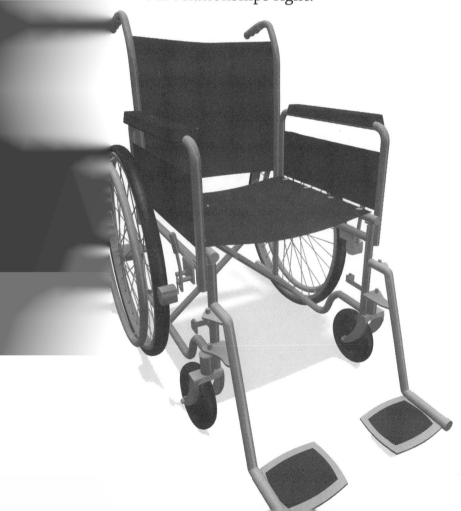

Like the lame man at the pool, we all wait "a long time" (verse 6) for something to happen that looks utterly out of reach. Sometimes our *whole lives* seem beyond our control.

It's natural to want others to do something for us. We can easily see why the lame man blamed his situation on others: *I have no one to help me!* Someone else always "steps down before me" (verse 7).

Could the lame man at the pool have stood and walked away carrying his mat if he hadn't met Jesus that day? Jesus came to him and changed everything. When the man couldn't even say who had healed him, Jesus came to him again.

Encountering Jesus again and again is the way we are made whole. We learn who he really is by being with him. But Jesus won't force himself on us. He respects our freedom to choose him or to choose someone or something else.

For one week, commit daily time to prayer so that you can encounter Jesus again and again. Set aside at least ten minutes a day, and ideally, twenty. Mark on your calendar a time and place where you won't be interrupted.

Morning is perfect because our minds haven't yet revved up for the day, but any time can work. You can even plan a different time each day. Remember, though, that it's difficult to be alert with God just before you fall asleep at night, so the earlier, the better. But no matter when you choose, make the commitment to be with Jesus, and then keep it! You might want to use a Scripture from Appendix D, "Suggested Scripture Passages for Prayer."

Even as Jesus saw the cured man in the temple, he sees you with love in his eyes. Allow him to find you by creating the time and place where you can be found during this week. Then talk to him, and listen.

All | In the name of
the Father, and
of the Son, and of
the Holy Spirit.
Amen.

Reader | Lord Jesus,
Thank you for our discussion tonight.
Thank you for the trust and respect we
have toward one another.
Help us to keep this commitment to
daily prayer for one week.
In our prayer, help us to listen with
expectant hearts,
That we may hear your still small voice.

Do a great work in us, O Lord,
for our need is great.
We don't want to live making excuses or
blaming others for our situations.
We want to be "unstuck," free.
Only you can do this, Jesus.
St. Paul said, "For freedom Christ has set
you free" (cf. Galatians 5:1).
We ask for that freedom in
your name, Jesus.
Give us the healing and new life
only you can offer.
Thank you, Jesus.

All | **Amen.**

A Sorrowful Woman

"I have
somthing
to say
to you."

Washes
Jesus' Feet

An extemporaneous prayer to the Holy Spirit to guide and inspire the discussion may be led by a group member or the leader.

In extemporaneous prayer, the person praying aloud talks to God on behalf of the group. Conclude the prayer with the **Glory Be** or the **Our Father**.

Share a time in your life when you were extremely thankful.

*Pharisees rigorously followed all the details of Jewish law. They confronted Jesus often because he and his followers did not obey the laws for ritual washing or those prohibiting Jews from eating, touching, or associating with sinners. In their view, Jesus also violated the laws governing the observance of the Sabbath.

Luke

[36]One of the Pharisees* asked him [Jesus] to eat with him, and he went into the Pharisee's house, and sat at table. [37]And behold, a woman of the city, who was a sinner, when she learned that he was sitting at table in the Pharisee's house, brought an alabaster flask of ointment, [38]and standing behind him at his feet, weeping, she began to wet his feet with her tears, and wiped them with the hair of her head, and kissed his feet, and anointed them with the ointment. [39]Now when the Pharisee who had invited him saw it, he said to himself, "If this man were a prophet, he would have known who and what sort of woman this is who is touching him, for she is a sinner." [40]And Jesus answering said to him, "Simon, I have something to say to you." And he answered, "What is it, Teacher?" [41]"A certain creditor had two debtors; one owed five hundred denarii,

7:36-50

and the other fifty. [42]When they could not pay, he forgave them both. Now which of them will love him more?" [43]Simon answered, "The one, I suppose, to whom he forgave more." And he said to him, "You have judged rightly." [44]Then turning toward the woman he said to Simon, "Do you see this woman? I entered your house, you gave me no water for my feet, but she has wet my feet with her tears and wiped them with her hair. [45]You gave me no kiss, but from the time I came in she has not ceased to kiss my feet. [46]You did not anoint my head with oil, but she has anointed my feet with ointment. [47]Therefore I tell you, her sins, which are many, are forgiven, for she loved much; but he who is forgiven little, loves little." [48]And he said to her, "Your sins are forgiven." [49]Then those who were at table with him began to say among themselves, "Who is this, who even forgives sins?" [50]And he said to the woman, "Your faith has saved you; go in peace."

1. Why might Simon the Pharisee have invited Jesus to his house, and why would Jesus have gone?

2. What do you think Luke means when he says that the woman who entered the house is a "sinner"?

3. What might have compelled the woman to interrupt a dinner party in order to make contact with Jesus?

4. How does Simon respond to the woman's washing of Jesus' feet?

5. What three ways did Jesus contrast Simon's hospitality with the woman's (verses 44-46)?

6. How do you think the woman felt when Jesus said to her, "Your sins are forgiven. . . . Your faith has saved you, go in peace" (verses 48, 50)?

7. What does the woman possess that Simon lacks? What would it take for him to have the same thing?

8. Do you identify most with Simon or with the woman? Why?

9. Have you ever had a sense of God being merciful and loving toward you, despite a particular failure, or many failures? How did that sense of mercy affect you?

10. The woman's actions pleased Jesus. What can we learn from her? How can this translate to our lives?

This week let the power of this story make a deepening impact on you. Spend time reading, studying, and meditating on Luke 7:36-50. Go a step further by imagining yourself in the scene at Simon's house.

God uses our imagination to communicate with us and plant ideas, images, and sometimes words. St. Ignatius of Loyola, founder of the Jesuits, taught that imaginative prayer with the Gospels leads to the greatest possible intimacy with God.

After you've read and thought about the story many times and know it well, imagine the physical scene in as much detail as you can: the temperature of the air, the appearance of the house, the food on the table, the people at the dinner. Fill in the picture as your mind wanders around the room. Ignatius calls this "composition of place." Whatever or whoever comes into your mind, even if it seems odd—sometimes especially if it seems odd—might be God communicating something to you.

Put yourself in the Gospel scene. Do you want to be the woman, Simon, an apostle, or an observing Pharisee? Trust that God will prompt your choice. Go through the action and dialogue as best you can remember it. Refer back to your Bible if you're not sure what happens next. Sometimes God uses this little memory lapse to draw your attention to something.

You need not follow the biblical script exactly. If you feel like asking Jesus a question, or Simon, or the woman, do it! Again, that could be Jesus prompting you. Pause in expectant anticipation of a response. If one of the characters says something unexpected, something not from the narrative, that could be a word from God for you.

The Catholic Mass is a way to offer ourselves to Jesus as the woman did. Anyone can attend a liturgy, including non-Catholics and non-Christians. At Mass we pray, "Lord, have mercy / Christ, have mercy / Lord, have mercy." We kneel before Jesus and tell him that we are not worthy. We hear him say that we are forgiven and that he wants to give us his peace.

Try attending Mass once this week on a weekday. Weekday liturgies have a completely different feel than Masses on Sundays. Experience it for yourself!

Read, or have someone else read this introduction:

The Holy Spirit responds to the world, revealing what we need when we need it. So many of us ache for God's loving mercy.

Early in the twentieth century, God responded by giving the Church a new devotion through a Polish nun, now known as St. Faustina. The devotion is called the "Chaplet of Divine Mercy." Pray it together (the words are included here). The Chaplet is usually prayed on one decade of rosary beads, but you don't need rosary beads to pray it. If this prayer touches you, you can learn more about the devotion online. A sung version is available on YouTube.

All | In the name of the Father, and of the Son, and of the Holy Spirit. **Amen.**

Reader Eternal Father, I offer You the Body and Blood, Soul and Divinity of Your dearly beloved Son, Our Lord Jesus Christ, in atonement for our sins and those of the whole world.

Reader For the sake of His sorrowful Passion,

All *have mercy on us and on the whole world.* (Repeat ten times.)

Reader Holy God, Holy Mighty One, Holy Immortal One,

All *have mercy on us and on the whole world.*

Reader Holy God, Holy Mighty One, Holy Immortal One,

All *have mercy on us and on the whole world.*

Reader Holy God, Holy Mighty One, Holy Immortal One,

All *have mercy on us and on the whole world.*

Jesus Raises Lazarus

**from
the Dead**

"The Teacher
is here and
is calling for
you."

John 11:28

Ask one person to read the following prayer.

All | In the name of the Father, and of the Son, and of the Holy Spirit. **Amen.**

Reader

A reading from the Book of the prophet Ezekiel.

Thus says the LORD God: Behold, I will open your graves,
and raise you from your graves, O my people;
and I will bring you home into the land of Israel.
And you shall know that I am the LORD,
when I open your graves,
and raise you from your graves, O my people.
And I will put my Spirit within you, and you shall live,
and I will place you in your own land;
then you shall know that I, the LORD, have spoken,
and I have done it, says the LORD. (37:12-14)

The word of the Lord.

All Thanks be to God.

Reader

Lord, as we reflect on and discuss your word,
we pray that you would open our minds and hearts.
Help us to desire greater faith and hope
in your power to work in our hearts.
Please use this time we have to strengthen our belief in you.
We pray this through Christ our Lord.

All Amen.

Is there a time when you have seen or experienced real and inspiring change, whether in yourself or another person?

John 11:1-6,

[1]Now a certain man was ill, Lazarus of Bethany, the village of Mary and her sister Martha. [2]It was Mary who anointed the Lord with ointment and wiped his feet with her hair, whose brother Lazarus was ill. [3]So the sisters sent to him, saying, "Lord, he whom you love is ill." [4]But when Jesus heard it he said, "This illness is not unto death; it is for the glory of God, so that the Son of God may be glorified by means of it."

[5]Now Jesus loved Martha and her sister and Lazarus. [6]So when he heard that he was ill, he stayed two days longer in the place where he was. . . . [14]Then Jesus told them plainly, "Lazarus is dead; [15]and for your sake I am glad that I was not there, so that you may believe. But let us go to him." . . .

4-15,17,20-29,32-44

[17]Now when Jesus came, he found that Lazarus had already been in the tomb four days. . . . [20]When Martha heard that Jesus was coming, she went and met him, while Mary sat in the house. [21]Martha said to Jesus, "Lord, if you had been here, my brother would not have died. [22]And even now I know that whatever you ask from God, God will give you." [23]Jesus said to her, "Your brother will rise again." [24] Martha said to him, "I know that he will rise again in the resurrection at the last day." [25]Jesus said to her, "I am the resurrection and the life; he who believes in me, though he die, yet shall he live, [26]and whoever lives and believes in me shall never die. Do you believe this?" [27]She said to him, "Yes, Lord;

I believe that you are the Christ, the Son of God, he who is coming into the world."

²⁸When she had said this, she went and called her sister Mary, saying quietly, "The Teacher is here and is calling for you." ²⁹And when she heard it, she rose quickly and went to him. . . . ³²Then Mary, when she came where Jesus was and saw him, fell at his feet, saying to him, "Lord, if you had been here, my brother would not have died." ³³When Jesus saw her weeping, and the Jews who came with her also weeping, he was deeply moved in spirit and troubled; ³⁴and he said, "Where have you laid him?" They said to him, "Lord, come and see." ³⁵Jesus wept. ³⁶So the Jews said, "See how he loved him!" ³⁷But some of them said, "Could not he who opened the eyes of the blind man have kept this man from dying?"

³⁸Then Jesus, deeply moved again, came to the tomb; it was a cave, and a stone lay upon it. ³⁹Jesus said, "Take away the stone." Martha, the sister of the dead man, said to him, "Lord, by this time there will be an odor, for he has been dead four days." ⁴⁰Jesus said to her, "Did I not tell you that if you would believe you would see the glory of God?" ⁴¹So they took away the stone. And Jesus lifted up his eyes and said, "Father, I thank thee that thou hast heard me. ⁴²I knew that thou hearest me always, but I have said this on account of the people standing by, that they may believe that thou didst send me." ⁴³When he had said this, he cried with a loud voice, "Lazarus, come out." ⁴⁴The dead man came out, his hands and feet bound with bandages, and his face wrapped with a cloth. Jesus said to them, "Unbind him, and let him go."

1. Describe the opening scene. Who is ill? Who communicates with Jesus? How are they identified?

2. How long does Jesus wait before going to Lazarus? How do you think Lazarus and his sisters felt about the delay? Why do you think he waits?

3. The first comment both Mary and Martha make when they see Jesus is the same (verses 21 and 32). What do they both say? What do you think they meant by their statements?

4. If you were Martha, how would you have felt about Jesus' statement in verse 23?

5. Describe Jesus' different emotions throughout this narrative. What seems to particularly move him?

6. Why do you think Jesus weeps?

7. In verse 40, Jesus says, "Did I not tell you that if you would believe you would see the glory of God?" What demonstrated Mary's and Martha's belief? What made this a demonstration of belief?

8. What action based on belief might the Lord be asking you to do in order to see his glory, as Mary and Martha did? What stone needs to be rolled away in your life?

You may read the following together if time allows, or go straight to "Encountering Christ for Life."

This week spend time reflecting on what binds you. Does anything in your life feel as hopeless or as inextricably bound or defeated as a dead body in a tomb, tightly wrapped and rotting for four days? Yet Jesus called Lazarus out of his tomb!

You may feel burdened, oppressed, or wrapped tightly by sins, wounds, or something else that prevents you from experiencing a closer relationship with Jesus. Reflect on your answer to the last question in this session: What stone do you want God to roll away? What is blocking your way in life?

Read through Scripture passages that call us to put Christ first, and pray through them. Some possibilities:

Philippians 3:7-14
Hebrews 12:1-3
Luke 9:23-26
Matthew 11:28-30
Ephesians 4:17-24
Galatians 5:1, 13-25

It's evident in these passages that Jesus wants freedom and new life for us! He doesn't want us feeling bound, oppressed, or even dead like Lazarus. To claim freedom and new life in him, we need to go to Jesus and ask him for it. He respects our freedom to choose him; he will never force himself on us.

One way for Catholics to reach out to Jesus for freedom and new life is in the Sacrament of Reconciliation, also known as Confession. Many people find the prospect a little frightening, which is natural and understandable. Sometimes, however, it simply helps to talk to a priest about our interior lives, the things that weigh us down or our resistance to following Jesus. That's what a priest is ordained by the Church to do!

Almost anyone who has experienced Confession finds that this sacrament has the power to roll away stones that separate us from one another and from God. Honestly sharing our struggles and hearing Jesus' love and forgiveness through the priest's words and prayers is an experience like no other.

If you feel too uneasy to seek this sacrament, talk to someone this week who has experienced sacramental reconciliation. Ask about the role this spiritual practice plays in his or her life. With this friend, talk and pray to seek understanding. The Church brings us together, and we as Church depend on one another to grow in faith.

If you're not Catholic, you can still talk to a priest, or to any ordained minister, about your struggles. Great comfort is available when we share the weight of our burdens with others, especially those, like the clergy, who are trained and experienced in helping fellow believers in their walk with the Lord.

If you've been to Confession or shared your struggles with a friend or someone in the clergy, try going to daily Mass afterward. Listen for Jesus speaking to you through the readings. If a sentence, word, or image stands out for you, God has drawn your attention to it for a reason. Ponder whatever you notice and talk to God about it.

If you're Catholic and have confessed any serious sin in the Sacrament of Reconciliation, ask Jesus to bring you newness of life through the Eucharist. The growth that you have experienced in this small group will be intensified by encountering Jesus sacramentally in his Body and Blood. When we wholeheartedly participate in the "source and summit" of the Catholic faith (as the Second Vatican Council called the Eucharist), we open ourselves to understanding the fullness Jesus offers to everyone: "I came that they may have life, and have it abundantly" (John 10:10).

Have someone read the following aloud; then discuss within the group.

Jesus raises Lazarus from the dead for at least two reasons: because **he loves him** *and* because Jesus wants his followers to see that he is **something more** than even the healer and exorcist they have already experienced.

Christians believe Jesus is one with God the Father (John 14:6-11), that he is the way our finite human understanding can experience the glory of God. Jesus has the power to free you, and he *wants* to free you so that you may personally experience his great love and power. He knows your need for healing draws you to seek him. He wants that, because he wants to be in a loving relationship with you, the kind of relationship he had with Martha, Mary, and Lazarus.

A relationship with Jesus rarely happens in isolation. Jesus commands the witnesses of the miracle to unbind Lazarus rather than rushing forward to tear the burial wrappings off of his beloved friend himself. Jesus may perform a miracle in your inner self and arrange for a community of believers to take part in your healing and freedom.

We were made for relationship, made in the image of God who is three in one—Father, Son, and Holy Spirit—an eternal community. We need consistent relationship with other Christians, prayer, and ongoing learning and formation in what is good, true, and beautiful. That is part of what unbinds us and sets us free.

This is not a one time event. Spiritual growth involves a commitment to daily prayer, praying with the Scriptures to allow God to speak to us, and regularly going to Mass as well as the Sacrament of Reconciliation. Some people also ask a trusted friend to help them learn the heart and habits of following Jesus closely. Or they may find someone trained in giving spiritual direction to help them grow.

But above anything else, allow the Spirit of the One who raised Lazarus from the grave to be your guide. Write down what he helps you decide to do going forward from this small group. That will help make concrete your commitment to continue seeking the Maker of heaven and earth.

Before closing with the following prayer, make the Sign of the Cross and pray extemporaneously for things that emerged from your discussion. Pray also for the needs of each person in your small group.

All | In the name of the Father, and of the Son, and of the Holy Spirit. **Amen.**

Reader | Thank you for this opportunity
to study your Word,
to discuss your way,
to seek the truth,
to encounter you in prayer.
Thank you for the friends we have
made through this group.

We have come to hope that you are the
resurrection and the life,
the One who knows and loves us,
who has the power to forgive us.

Change us like Zacchaeus,
heal us like Bartimaeus,
forgive us like the woman
who washed your feet,
unbind us like Lazarus.
Set us free!
Please guide us to greater healing,
forgiveness, and freedom.

We pray in your name,
"the name which is above every name, . . .
the name of Jesus" (Philippians 2:9, 10).
May it ever be on our lips and in our hearts.

All | **Amen.**

Appendices for Participants

Appendix

A small group seeks to foster an honest exploration of Jesus Christ with one another. For many, this will be a new experience. You may be wondering what will take place. Will I fit in? Will I even want to come back?

Here are some expectations and values to help participants understand how small groups work as well as what makes them work and what doesn't. When a group meets for the first time, the facilitator may want to read the following aloud and discuss it to be sure people understand small group parameters.

Purpose
We gather as searchers. Our express purpose for being here is to explore together what it means to live the gospel of Jesus Christ in and through the Church.

Priority
In order to reap the full fruit of this personal and communal journey, each one of us will make participation in the weekly gatherings a priority.

Participation
We will strive to create an environment in which all are encouraged to share at their comfort level.

Discussion Guidelines
The purpose of our gathering time is to share in "Spirit-filled" discussion. This type of dialogue occurs when the presence of the Holy Spirit is welcomed and

encouraged by the nature and tenor of the discussion. To help this happen, we will observe the following guidelines:

- Participants strive always to be respectful, humble, open, and honest in listening and sharing: they don't interrupt, respond abruptly, condemn what another says, or even judge in their hearts.

- Participants share at the level that is comfortable for them personally.

- Silence is a vital part of the experience. Participants are given time to reflect before discussion begins. Keep in mind that a period of comfortable silence often occurs between individuals speaking.

- Participants are enthusiastically encouraged to share while at the same time exercising care to permit others (especially the quieter members) an opportunity to speak. Each participant should aim to maintain a balance: participating without dominating the conversation.

- Participants keep confidential anything personal that may be shared in the group.

- Perhaps most important, participants should cultivate attentiveness to the Holy Spirit's desire to be present in the time spent together. When the conversation seems to need help, ask for the Holy Spirit's intercession silently in your heart. When someone is speaking of something painful or difficult, pray that the Holy Spirit comforts that person. Pray for the Spirit to aid the group to respond sensitively and lovingly. If someone isn't participating, praying for that person during silence may be more helpful than a direct question. These are but a few examples of the ways in which each person might personally invoke the Holy Spirit.

Time

It is important that your group start and end on time. Generally a group meets for about ninety minutes, with an additional thirty minutes or so afterwards for refreshments. Agree on these times as a group and work to honor them.

Appendix  B

Once God gets our attention, we often find ourselves wanting more. Just as often, we don't have the first idea about how to seek God on our own without the support of our small group.

Catholic tradition contains a treasure trove of spiritual riches on which to draw. This appendix offers a variety of means by which to come to know Jesus more deeply: discussing Scripture with a friend, reading the Bible, and reading the writings of the saints and spiritual teachers. Skim to find what appeals to your heart.

For a Discussion with a Christian Friend

Please read Hebrews 4:12 together and discuss the following questions:

1. What does the metaphor "sharper than any two-edged sword" mean to you?

2. Why would the word of God penetrate "soul and spirit, joints and marrow"? What do you think the writer of Hebrews wants you to understand by this image/metaphor?

3. Can you explain in practical terms how the word of God judges the reflections and thoughts of the heart?

4. Have you ever experienced the word of God becoming "living" to you, touching your heart and mind to convert you, even if it was about something minor?

5. Do you ever turn to the word of God in times when you don't have anywhere else to turn? What have been the results?

6. What challenges have you had with Scripture? How have you been able to work through them?

Getting to Know Christ through the Bible

1. A pen and paper can make the difference between reading the Bible and really meditating on it—considering the story or teaching deeply in order to become more familiar with Jesus.

2. Write down observations about the text as you read and record questions that come to your mind, either in the margins of your Bible or in a journal.

3. Look up cross-references if your Bible has them, or look online, especially if they relate to your questions. Record your insights.

4. Find a key word in your text that interests you and use an online concordance to review where else it appears. Read those other passages to deepen your understanding of the meaning of that word. Note your feelings.

5. For those who are more visual, draw a picture inspired by a Scripture story.

6. Summarize in writing what happened in the Scripture passage you read, or what the writer was saying.

The Three Essentials for a Rich Experience of God through Scripture: Memorize, Meditate, and Apply

Memorize

We may think that memorization is tedious and a waste of time, but that's not true. Having the words of Jesus or his followers readily at hand can be an important step in getting to know him. When you really come to know a friend, you will sometimes think, "I know what 'Joe' would say in this situation." This is also the case with Jesus. As you come to know him better, you'll want to be able to recall something he has said, because as you do, you will feel his presence more intensely. But you can only do this if you have memorized his words.

If you know it by heart, Scripture is available to you anytime, anywhere, day or night, whether you are free or imprisoned, healthy or sick, walking with a friend, or sitting quietly before the Eucharist.

Here are some techniques to help you with memorization:

1. Memorizing is much more fruitful after you've meditated on a passage. (See instructions for meditation below.)

2. Memorize steadily for a few days rather than cramming all at once. You will retain the information longer, and meditating on it will give you time to consider what is being said.

3. Continue to review the words you have memorized, or you will lose them. One of the best times to do this is right before you

fall asleep. At bedtime you don't need the fresh mind necessary for new memorization.

Meditate

Meditation is deep thinking on the teachings and spiritual realities in Scripture for the purposes of understanding, application, and prayer. A short description could be "absorption," "focused attention," or "intense consideration."

Meditation goes beyond hearing, reading, studying, or even memorizing. Instead, it is a means of absorbing the words and allowing God to speak to you through them.

Both Jews and Christians have attested that *God uses Scripture to speak to us.* When we make ourselves available to God mentally and spiritually in this way, he will reach us through his word.

God is gentle and gracious—he will never force us. Rather, he continuously invites us. When we give the time and attention that meditation requires, God in return gives us all the gifts a loving father longs to give his children.

Start with verses that conspicuously relate to your own concerns and personal needs. These can be found easily on any Internet search engine. (For example, search "Scripture passages on anxiety" or "Bible verses on seeking God's strength.") Through Scriptures relevant to your life, God can meet your needs very quickly. He wants our communication with Jesus to be rooted in the Scriptures.

Some tips and methods for meditation:

1. Summarize in your own words what the passage is saying, or what happens in what order in a narrative or dialogue.

- You can do this in your head, but it's even better if you jot it down in a journal. This is an extremely useful practice. Some of us think we know the Scriptures because they are proclaimed in church, particularly the Gospels. When we try to summarize in the order of events/dialogue, however, we learn how much we have been missing!

- Don't worry about trying to summarize from memory—you should go back to the text to clarify. Sometimes observing that you have glossed over verses can be an indication that you need to spend time on a particular teaching.

2. Talk to Jesus about the Scripture passage you are reading.

- By talking to Jesus, you submit your mind to the Holy Spirit's illumination of the text and intensify your spiritual perception.

- Allow time both for both reading and talking to Jesus. If you rush through the reading, you won't retain anything. If you say a few words to Jesus and then dash off, you aren't really giving him time to speak or explain things to you. Think how much you retain or receive when you're rushed in speaking to another person. It's the same with God!

3. Don't bite off more than you can chew. Better to read and consider a few verses or a short passage than to ingest big chunks without meditation.

Apply

If we do something about what we have read, what we read is incorporated into our lives as it can be in no other way. "Be doers of the word, and not hearers only, deceiving yourselves" (James 1:22). An application is a concrete step you can take in response to your prayer and meditation.

1. Expect to find an application—open the Bible in anticipation of discovering what you need!

2. Meditate to discern an application. Meditation isn't an end in itself. It leads to inner transformation, and inner transformation comes from and leads to action.

3. Sometimes an action step is so evident that it jumps off the page. If this doesn't happen, be sure to ask questions of the text that orient you towards action. For example:

- Does this text reveal something I should believe?

- Does this text reveal something I should praise or thank or trust God for?

- Does this text reveal something I should pray about for myself and others?

- Does this text reveal something about which I should have a new attitude?

- Does this text reveal something about which I should make a decision?

- Does this text reveal something I should do for the sake of Christ and others or myself?

Commit to one specific response. Less is more if you really do it.

Scripture reading and meditation techniques are necessary because we all need to prevent shallow reading. Modern technology forms us for fast and superficial communication. In fact, we often talk to others shallowly because our attention is on texting, tweeting, the next thing we're doing—the list is endless!

We must fight this tendency for the sake of our humanity. In one episode of an old sci-fi television show, the original *Star Trek*, the former inhabitants of another planet had continually sped up, ultimately moving so fast that they became merely buzzing sounds. When they invaded the starship *Enterprise*, the crew thought that flies had come in with the food supplies. These aliens had lost their very beings because they valued speed above all else.

Watch to see if you're reading Scripture hurriedly or in a perfunctory way because you think you should, not because you are seeking to meet God there.

If Jesus met you on the street today, do you think he would be shallow, half listening, rushing, or distracted? Can these be the ways of a loving God? If not, then they can't be the way of a loving person either! Remember, Christ is those "other people" you will meet on the street and everywhere you go each day. Loving attention to God in Scripture forms us for loving attention to others.

Spiritual Reading

The Church has consistently valued the witness of the communion of saints. We are fortunate that as Catholics, we have a rich tradition of stories of holy men and women whose lives have witnessed to their great love of God and others. In addition, many saints canonized by the Church, as well as other spiritual teachers, have left written or artistic works that the Church recognizes as invaluable tools for coming to know God.

Perhaps—especially if you were raised Catholic—you already have an interest in a specific saint or spiritual teacher. If so, find out if that saint has left any written or artistic works. Either can be used to consider Jesus. Or ask a friend about saints whose writings have helped them. Biographies of the lives of saints and Christian heroes can also be inspiring reading.

Spiritual reading is much like Scripture meditation. If we read quickly and do not consider what we have read, nothing much sticks. If we read slowly and allow time to think about what we have read, then we absorb it. God communicates with us through considered reading.

Scripture reading with meditation holds priority over spiritual reading because Christians have always taught that the Scriptures are the privileged means by which God works in our hearts and minds. That is why Christians encourage daily reading of Scripture above any other spiritual reading. The saints and spiritual teachers enlighten and inspire us for the reading of Scripture.

The Evangelical Catholic recommends reading and meditating on Scripture in the morning, when you are fresh, or during a break in your day. You can save the spiritual reading for later on, either in the evening or at bedtime.

Writings of the Saints and Christian Teachers

Some classics that have helped those seeking to know Christ:

The Way of Perfection by Teresa of Avila. This is the best book to begin with when reading St. Teresa. A Doctor of the Church, Teresa is loved by many for her writings on prayer and the spiritual life. This book is short and simple. Teresa's direct language and folksy style make for a particularly engaging read.

Autobiography of Teresa of Avila, also called *The Story of Her Life.* This is longer than *The Way of Perfection* and includes St. Teresa's famous metaphor on prayer as a garden. Read this when you're ready for extended time with St. Teresa.

The Story of a Soul, also called *The Autobiography of St. Thérèse of Lisieux* . In surveys on favorite saints, St. Thérèse consistently tops the list. She speaks in her memoir with an unaffected, honest voice, almost like the voice of a child. She died as a cloistered Carmelite nun at the age of twenty-four, but despite her young age, she was soon recognized as a spiritual giant. St. Thérèse is known for her "little way" of humble love. For first-time readers, her little way may appear simple or silly. But once you try it, you learn that loving sacrificially, like Jesus, truly does require you to lose our life in order to save it.

Introduction to the Devout Life by St. Francis de Sales. This is a great read for beginners because it has so much direction on how to live as a follower of Jesus. You can read each short and accessible chapter in only ten to fifteen minutes. Reading one each day will give you plenty of real spiritual meat to chew on.

Pensées by Blaise Pascal. This classic has influenced countless Christians. Pascal was a seventeenth-century mathematician. The *pensées*, or "thoughts," are scattered fragments of his theological and philosophical ponderings after his conversion to Christianity.

New Seeds of Contemplation and *No Man Is an Island* by Thomas Merton. Merton is widely considered one of the greatest spiritual writers of the twentieth century. His compartmentalized prose provides quick, sophisticated reading "nuggets" capable of leading you into profound thoughts on God. The language of his later works is more accessible than those of his earlier ones.

The Confessions of Saint Augustine. This well-loved classic details Augustine's search for God. The immediacy of his struggle to believe is evident and something every person, even today, can relate to. Augustine's conversion story finishes with Book 9. The later chapters are written as a long disquisition on time and memory. This is rich stuff, but it's not for every reader.

The Imitation of Christ by Thomas à Kempis. Apart from the Bible, no book has been translated into more languages than this classic. It was a favorite of Teresa of Avila, Thomas More, Ignatius of Loyola (founder of the Jesuits), Thérèse of Lisieux, and countless saints and Christians of other denominations, including John Wesley and John Newton, founders of the Methodist movement. The book has remained popular because of its profound insights about human nature and the struggle to live a holy life.

Autobiography of Saint Ignatius of Loyola. This short description of St. Ignatius' famous conversion from a womanizing soldier to a Christian mendicant, or beggar, is both a classic and an easy read. The story includes Ignatius' observations on his interior life while convalescing from serious war wounds. These become not only the immediate cause of his conversion but also the groundwork for his thought on the discernment of spirits in his *Spiritual Exercises.*

The Long Loneliness by Dorothy Day. Day was a worldly young communist in the heyday of early twentieth-century social movements. She lived in New York City as many young women live today: taking lovers, having an abortion, and promoting a secular salvation through political change. After her conversion to Catholicism, Day founded the Catholic Worker movement, still in existence today, to offer hospitality to Christ in the poor and needy. Simply written and very moving, Day's is one of the great conversion stories of the last century.

Appendix  C

If it has been a long time since you last went to Confession—or if you've never been—you may be hesitant and unsure. Don't let these very common feelings get in your way. Reconciling with God and the Church always brings great joy. Take the plunge—you will be glad you did!

If it will help to alleviate your fears, familiarize yourself with the step-by-step description of the process below. Most priests are happy to help anyone willing to take the risk. If you forget anything, the priest will remind you. So don't worry about committing every step and word to memory. Remember, Jesus isn't giving you a test; he just wants you to experience the grace of his mercy!

Catholics believe that the priest acts *in persona Christi,* "in the person of Christ." The beauty of the sacraments is that they touch us both physically and spiritually. On the physical level in Confession, we hear the words of absolution through the person of the priest. On the spiritual level, we know that it is Christ assuring us that he has truly forgiven us. We are made clean!

You usually have the option of going to Confession anonymously—in a confessional booth or in a room with a screen—or face-to-face with the priest. Whatever your preference will be fine with the priest.

Steps in the Sacrament of Reconciliation:

1. Prepare to receive the sacrament by praying and examining your conscience. If you need help, you can

find many different lists of questions online that will help you examine your conscience.

2. Once you're with the priest, begin by making the Sign of the Cross while greeting the priest with these words: "Bless me, Father, for I have sinned." Then tell him how long it has been since your last confession. If it's your first confession, tell him so.

3. Confess your sins to the priest. If you are unsure about anything, ask him to help you. Place your trust in God, who is a merciful and loving Father.

4. When you are finished, indicate this by saying, "I am sorry for these and all of my sins." Don't worry later that you forgot something. This closing statement covers everything that didn't come to mind in the moment. Trust God that he has brought to mind what he wanted you to address.

5. The priest will assign you a penance, such as a prayer, a Scripture reading, or a work of mercy, service, or sacrifice.

6. Express sorrow for your sins by saying an Act of Contrition. Many versions of these prayers can be found online. If memorization is difficult for you, just say you're sorry in your own words.

7. The priest, acting again in the person of Christ, will absolve you of your sins with prayerful words, ending with, "I absolve you from your sins in the name of the Father, and of the Son, and of the Holy Spirit." You respond by making the Sign of the Cross and saying, "Amen."

8. The priest will offer some proclamation of praise, such as "Give thanks to the Lord, for he is good" (from Psalm 136). You can respond, "His mercy endures forever."

9. The priest will dismiss you.

10. Be sure to complete your assigned penance immediately or as soon as possible.

Luke 11:9-13: Good gifts from a good father

Luke 15:11-32: Parable of the Lost Son

John 14:1-6, 15-21, 25-27: Jesus' words of comfort at the Last Supper

Jeremiah 29:11-14: Words of encouragement to the Israelites in exile

Psalm 23: The Lord is our shepherd

Romans 8:31-39: Nothing can separate us from the love of God

2 Corinthians 4:7-18: Encouragement in trial and weakness

Philippians 4:4-9: Encouragement to rejoice, pray, and be at peace

Ephesians 3:14-21: Prayer to be filled with the fullness of God

Psalm 16: Prayer of trust in the Lord's security

Song of Songs 2:10-14: Words of the Lord, our Lover

Isaiah 43:1-7: Promises of redemption and restoration

Appendices for Facilitators

E The Role of the Facilitator

F A Guide for Each Session of *Believe*

G Leading Prayer and "Encountering Christ This Week"

Appendix  E

Perhaps no skill is more important to the success of a small group than the ability to facilitate a discussion lovingly. It is God's Holy Spirit working through our personal spiritual journey, not necessarily our theological knowledge, that makes this possible.

The following guidelines can help facilitators avoid some of the common pitfalls of small group discussion. The goal is to open the door for the Spirit to take the lead and guide your every response because you are attuned to his movements.

Pray daily and before your small group meeting. This is the only way you can learn to sense the Spirit's gentle promptings when they come!

You are a Facilitator, Not a Teacher

As a facilitator, it can be extremely tempting to answer every question. You may have excellent answers and be excited about sharing them with your brothers and sisters in Christ. However, a more Socratic method, by which you attempt to draw answers from participants, is much more fruitful for everyone else and for you as well.

Get in the habit of reflecting participants' questions or comments to the whole group before offering your own input. It is not necessary for you as a facilitator to enter immediately into the discussion or to offer a magisterial answer. When others have sufficiently addressed an issue, try to exercise restraint in your comments. Simply affirm what has been said; then thank them and move on.

If you don't know the answer to a question, have a participant look it up in the *Catechism of the Catholic Church* and read it aloud to the group. If you cannot find an answer, ask someone to research the question for the next session. Never feel embarrassed to say, "I don't know." Simply acknowledge the quality of the question and offer to follow up with that person after you have done some digging. Remember, you are a facilitator, not a teacher.

Affirm and Encourage

We are more likely to repeat a behavior when it is openly encouraged. If you want more active participation and sharing, give positive affirmation to the responses of the group members. This is especially important if people are sharing from their hearts. A simple "Thank you for sharing that" can go a long way in encouraging further discussion in your small group.

If someone has offered a theologically questionable response, don't be nervous or combative. Wait until others have offered their input. It is very likely that someone will proffer a more helpful response, which you can affirm by saying something such as, "That is the Christian perspective on that topic. Thank you."

If no acceptable response is given and you know the answer, exercise great care and respect in your comments so as not to appear smug or self-righteous. You might begin with something such as, "Those are all interesting perspectives. What the Church has said about this is . . . "

Avoid Unhelpful Tangents

Nothing can derail a Spirit-filled discussion more quickly than digressing on unnecessary tangents. Try to keep the session on track. If conversation strays from the topic, ask yourself, "Is this a

Spirit-guided tangent?" Ask the Holy Spirit too! If not, bring the group back by asking a question that steers conversation to the Scripture passage or to a question you have been discussing. You may even suggest kindly, "Have we gotten a little off topic?" Most participants will respond positively and get back on track through your sensitive leading.

That being said, some tangents may be worth pursuing if you sense a movement of the Spirit. It may be exactly where God wants to steer the discussion. You will find that taking risks can yield some beautiful results.

Don't Fear the Silence

Be okay with silence. Most people need a moment or two to come up with a response to a question. People naturally require some time to formulate their thoughts and put them into words. Some may need a few moments just to gather the courage to speak at all.

Regardless of the reason, don't be afraid of a brief moment of silence after asking a question. Let everyone in the group know early on that silence is an integral part of normal small group discussion. They needn't be anxious or uncomfortable when it happens. God works in silence!

This applies to times of prayer as well. If no one shares or prays after a sufficient amount of time, just move on gracefully.

The Power of Hospitality

A little hospitality can go far in creating community. Everybody likes to feel cared for. This is especially true in a small group whose purpose it is to connect to Jesus Christ, a model for care, support, and compassion.

Make a point to greet people personally when they first arrive. Ask them how their day has been going. Take some time to invest in the lives of your small group participants. Pay particular attention to newcomers. Work at remembering each person's name. Help everyone feel comfortable and at home. Allow your small group to be an environment where authentic relationships take shape and blossom.

Encourage Participation

Help everyone to get involved, especially those who are naturally less vocal or outgoing. To encourage participation initially, always invite various group members to read aloud the selected readings. Down the road, even after the majority of the group feels comfortable sharing, you may still have some quieter members who rarely volunteer a response to a question but would be happy to read.

Meteorology?

Keep an eye on the "Holy Spirit barometer." Is the discussion pleasing to the Holy Spirit? Is this conversation leading participants to a deeper personal connection to Jesus Christ? The intellectual aspects of our faith are certainly important to discuss, but conversation can sometimes degenerate into an unedifying showcase of intellect and ego. Other times discussion becomes an opportunity for gossip, detraction, complaining, or even slander. When this happens, you can almost feel the Holy Spirit leaving the room!

If you are aware that this dynamic has taken over a discussion, take a moment to pray quietly in your heart. Ask the Holy Spirit to help you bring the conversation to a more wholesome topic. This can often be achieved simply by moving to the next question.

Pace

Generally, you want to pace the session to finish in the allotted time, but sometimes this may be impossible without sacrificing quality discussion. If you reach the end of your meeting and find that you have covered only half the material, don't fret! This is often the result of lively Spirit-filled discussion and meaningful theological reflection.

In such a case, you may take time at another meeting to cover the remainder of the material. If you have only a small portion left, you can ask participants to pray through these on their own and come to the following meeting with any questions or insights they might have. Even if you must skip a section to end on time, make sure you leave adequate time for prayer and to review the "Encounter Christ This Week" section. This is vital in helping participants integrate their discoveries from the group into their daily lives.

Genuine Friendships

The best way to show Jesus' love and interest in your small group members is to meet with them for coffee, dessert, or a meal outside of your small group time.

You can begin by suggesting that the whole group get together for ice cream or some other social event at a different time than when your small group usually meets. Socializing will allow relationships to develop. It provides the opportunity for different kinds of conversations than small group sessions allow. You will notice an immediate difference in the quality of community in your small group at the next meeting.

After that first group social, try to meet one-on-one with each person in your small group. This allows for more in-depth conversation and personal sharing, giving you the chance to know each participant better so that you can love and care for them as Jesus would.

Jesus called the twelve apostles in order that they could "be with him" (Mark 3:14). When people spend time together, eat together, laugh together, cry together, and talk about what matters to them, intense Christian community develops. That is the kind of community Jesus was trying to create, and that must be the kind of community we try to create, because it changes lives. And changed lives change the world!

Joy
Remember that seeking the face of the Lord brings joy! Nothing is more fulfilling, more illuminating, and more beautiful than fostering a deep and enduring relationship with Jesus Christ. Embrace your participants and the entire spiritual journey with a spirit of joyful anticipation of what God wants to accomplish.

"These things I have spoken to you, that my joy may be in you, and that your joy may be full." (John 15:11)

Appendix F

God can respond to us personally through the Scriptures, no matter how much knowledge we have of biblical times. But God can also speak to us through commonly known information about the social and religious situations at the time that Jesus lived. The following notes will help you assist your group to better understand the Scriptures you read each week.

The notes for Week 1 include suggestions for ways to help people become comfortable, while the notes for Week 6 provide ideas for encouraging participants to go forward in a deeper life in Christ. Review the notes as you prepare for each session.

Week 1
Zacchaeus

Everyone in your small group may not know one another. The first time you meet, set people at ease by asking a few questions. You can use the ones we have suggested below, or formulate your own.

In choosing questions, it's important that they have no right or wrong answer; choose topics about which no one could feel that their answer is the only right one. Be sure to avoid anything controversial. During this process, ask people to share their names. Here are some sample questions:

- Who is the greatest quarterback in the NFL?

- What do you think is the best way to spend a vacation?

Here are some examples of responses:

- "I'm Greg. I'm a freshman in _____ dorm and a friend of _____. He made me come! I think that Peyton Manning is the greatest quarterback the NFL has ever seen or ever will!"

- "I'm Leslie, mother of three and a parishioner at St Luke's. The best way I could spend a vacation is to have a full-time nanny for a week—anywhere."

Scripture Discussion

If the discussion of the Scripture passage doesn't adequately convey the contempt in which the Jews held tax collectors, draw out that point through some questions. For example, how would you feel if the U.S. were occupied by another nation and someone from the parish or campus ministry demanded a contribution plus extra money for himself? (Explain that tax collectors paid their own wages by extorting above and beyond the taxes Rome levied.)

The Roman Empire is a fascinating topic, but avoid allowing the session to become a history lesson. A certain number of facts expand our understanding of what is happening; too many make your small group a class, not a group that seeks to encounter Christ together.

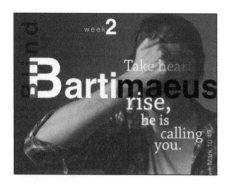

Week 2
Blind Bartimaeus

Scripture Discussion

The Jewish people believed that those who suffered from serious physical ailments (like congenital blindness) were being punished for sin, either their own sin or that of their parents.

It will likely come up, but if after a little discussion no one mentions the suffering that Bartimaeus has endured, ask questions to draw out what Bartimaeus' life would have been like and the possible effects those circumstances could have on a person.

Closing Prayer

If possible, spend a few minutes in extemporaneous prayer before reading St. Augustine's prayer to close the session.

If you gauge that your group members are unaccustomed to prayers such as Augustine's or are unaccustomed to the kind of language he uses, you could ask them questions about it as you socialize afterwards or prepare to leave. For example, ask what they thought of the prayer and if any words or phrases struck them, encouraged them, or confused them.

Week 3
Jesus Teaches about Worry and Anxiety

This session covers a topic of interest to almost everyone. It suggests memorizing a short Scripture passage. If you're a person who already memorizes Scripture, good for you! If not, try memorizing the recommended verse, or another, in advance of the meeting. You will experience the fruits of having the word of God readily at hand when you need it. This will allow you to testify to the power of this practice for help in following Jesus more closely.

This session casually mentions that Catholics can take worry and anxiety to the Sacrament of Reconciliation. If people respond with fear or incomprehension, it's a great opportunity to witness to the power of the sacrament in your own spiritual life. Tell the group that you will talk more about this sacrament in Session 6.

week **4**

at the **Pool**

Healing

Do you want to be healed?

John 5:6

Week 4
Healing at the Pool

In this story of the healing at the sheep pool at Bethesda, we read the term "the Jews." This is terminology John uses frequently in his Gospel to describe the Jewish religious and political leadership, not all Jews. Jesus was Jewish, as were his mother, Mary, and his first close followers, the apostles.

When describing the same scene as John describes, the synoptic gospels (Matthew, Mark, and Luke) call the Jewish leaders by their offices or beliefs: "chief priest," "Sadducees," "scribes," "Pharisees," and "elders." For an example of this, compare the stories of the cleansing of the temple in John 2:13-25 and Matthew 21:12-13.

Someone in your group might observe that this Scripture passage and John's Gospel in general appear to be anti-Semitic. Should that happen, explain that John's Gospel was written at a time when Christians had already been expelled from the synagogues, causing enmity between followers of Jesus and the Jewish leadership.

In AD 70, the Romans decimated Jerusalem and destroyed the temple. Jewish leaders sought to maintain their religion when the temple sacrifices, offerings, and observances could no longer be made. The post-temple rabbinic Judaism we know today was formed to keep the Jewish faith from being destroyed along with the temple. This involved the condemnation of any practices, like Judaic Christianity, that seemed to diverge from what the Jewish leadership believed was essential to Judaism.

Much more could be said on this topic. You don't want to allow your time seeking Christ to be derailed by extensive discussion of historical forces that shaped the Gospel of John. This information should be summarized as briefly as possible. Discussion of issues raised by anti-Semitism can certainly happen if people wish, but keep it brief. Encourage further discussion during the social time if group members seem to have more to say on the topic.

Week 5
A Sorrowful Woman Washes Jesus' Feet

The "Encountering Christ This Week" section of this session in- cludes a suggestion to attend Mass during the week. You might want to try doing this together as a group. If the daily Mass sched- ule conflicts with the responsibilities of some of the group mem- bers, it may work better to decide to meet for a Sunday Mass and then go out to breakfast afterward.

Spending time together outside of your small group meeetings allows greater intimacy to develop. It provides the chance to talk with others one-on-one to learn more about their personal history. Read more on this in Appendix E, "The Role of the Facilitator."

Week 6
Jesus Raises Lazarus from the Dead

Week 6 includes both an "Encountering Christ This Week" rec-ommendation and an "Encountering Christ for Life" section to conclude your small group. You can ask the group if they're willing to spend fifteen or twenty minutes extra at this last session in order to discuss the ideas we present about taking the gifts and revelations of this small group forward into life. Or if that is not possible, you can skip "Encountering Christ This Week" in order to end at the same time while still discussing how to go forward.

If you skip "Encountering Christ This Week," strongly encourage everyone to do the recommended prayer and reflection on their own during the week. This will help seal the group's conversation on the Scripture passage and deepen each person's encounter with Christ from the discussion.

You should also mention that "Encountering Christ This Week" suggests that each person seek out the Sacrament of Reconciliation and describes it more fully than in Week 3. Read this yourself in advance so that you will be prepared to summarize the content. Make it clear that this sacrament is for our freedom and consolation, not for condemnation, and point out that Appendix C outlines the process for going to Confession.

Your group may decide that they want to continue meeting. That would be a gift from God and a tribute to your ability to facilitate well and create a loving community! The Evangelical Catholic has other small group guides that you could use for discussion, as do many other organizations. Or you could work through a book of the Bible together. If you decide to explore the Bible together, you can find many books and online resources on how to ask questions of the text that lead to fruitful discussion.

No matter whether you continue meeting or not, thank the group for the time they have given and the commitment they have shown. It's a great honor to walk with people on their spiritual journeys. Share that sentiment if you are moved to do so!

Try to have a more celebratory atmosphere at this last session by providing a dessert or other treat for the social time. Maybe you can ask members to bring something to share.

Appendix  G

Opening Prayer

We have purposefully provided a guided opening prayer in most sessions because it can help people who are completely new to small groups and shared prayer to feel more at ease. If everyone or most people present are already comfortable with group prayer, involve them during subsequent gatherings.

As a facilitator, your goal is to provide opportunities for everyone to grow in leading prayer. After the first meeting, tell the group that you will allow time at the end of your prayer for others to voice their hopes for the group's time together. By Week 3, you could invite other people to open the group with prayer.

If you are comfortable leading an extemporaneous opening prayer, feel free to do that as soon as you wish. In "Week 1: Zacchaeus," you could skip the prayer we have provided after the psalm to pray in your own words instead. This would be ideal since some people have never witnessed spontaneous prayer. Such prayer demonstrates how to talk to God from the heart; it also expands the group's understanding of who God is and the relationship we can have with Jesus Christ.

You could begin any week by praising and thanking the Lord for the gift of gathering together. Thank God for giving each person present the desire to sacrifice their time to attend the group. You could ask the Holy Spirit to help open hearts and illuminate minds to the Scripture passages you'll be reading. Ask the Holy Spirit to guide the discussion so that you can all grow from it.

End by saying something such as, "We pray this through Christ our Lord" or "We pray this in Jesus' name," and then end with the Sign of the Cross.

Some essentials for extemporaneous prayer:

- Speak in the first-person plural "we." For example, "Holy Spirit, *we* ask you to open *our* hearts . . . " It's fine to add a line asking the Holy Spirit to help you facilitate the discussion as he wills, or something else to that effect, but most of the prayer should be for the whole group.

- Model speaking directly to Jesus our Lord. This may sound obvious, but among Catholic laypeople, it isn't frequently practiced or modeled. This is a very evangelical thing to do in the sense that it witnesses to the gospel. Not only does it show how much the Lord loves us, but it also demonstrates our confidence that he listens to us. As we say our Lord's name, we remind ourselves, as well as those who hear us, that we aren't just talking to ourselves. This builds up our faith. Those unaccustomed to hearing someone pray in this way may feel a bit uncomfortable at first, but they will quickly become more comfortable as they hear such prayers repeatedly. Remember, many graces come from praying "the name above every other name" (cf. Philippians 2:9). If you've never publicly prayed to Jesus, you may feel childish at first, but pray for the humility of a child. After all, Jesus said that we needed to become like children (Matthew 18:3)! The more we pray directly to Jesus in our own personal prayer life, the less awkward it will feel when we pray to him publicly.

- Model great trust that the Lord hears your prayer and will answer it. It's terrific just to say in prayer, "Jesus, we trust you!"

- Close by inviting all to join in a prayer of the Church, such as a the Glory Be, the Our Father, or the Hail Mary. This will bring all into the prayer.

Closing Prayer

For the closing prayer, we recommend that you always model extemporaneous prayer, even if we have provided a prayer. There is no other way to address the thoughts, concerns, and inspirations that come up in your group. Some sessions include topic suggestions based on the Scripture passage discussed, but praying about what was said is far preferable.

If your group members are comfortable praying aloud, invite others to join in the closing prayer in the first week. If not, wait another week or two. Once you feel that they are ready, invite them to participate. You could tell the group that you will begin the closing prayer and then allow for silence so that they can also pray aloud. Make sure they know that you will close the group's prayer by leading them into an Our Father after everyone is done praying spontaneously. This structure helps people feel comfortable offering their own prayers.

If a group is new to prayer, it might help to wait several weeks before inviting participants to pray aloud so that they have time to feel at ease about it. What follows are some possible ways to begin this process. However, don't read these suggestions verbatim—put them into your own words. It's not conducive to helping people become comfortable praying aloud if you are praying out of a book.

"The closing prayer is a great time to take the reflections we've shared, bring them to God, and ask him to help us make any inspirations a reality in our lives. God doesn't care about how well-spoken or articulate we are when we pray, so we shouldn't either! We don't judge each other's prayers. Let's pray from our hearts, knowing that God hears and cares about what we say, not how perfectly we say it. When we pray something aloud, we know that the Holy Spirit is mightily at work within us because it's the Spirit who gives us the courage to speak. God helps us lift up our hearts."

"Tonight for closing prayer, let's each voice our needs to one another; then we will take turns putting our right hand on the shoulder of the person to the right of us and praying for that person. After we each express our prayer needs, I will start by praying for Karen on my right. That means that I need to listen carefully when she tells us what she needs prayer for. We may not remember everyone's needs, so be sure to listen well to the person on your right. I'll voice my prayer needs first; then we'll go around the circle to the right. Okay? Does anyone have any questions?"

Encountering Christ This Week

These weekly prayer and reflection exercises are critical to allowing Jesus to enter more fully into the hearts of you and your small group members. If we don't give God the time that allows him to work in us, we experience far less fruit from our small group discussions. Prayer and reflection water the seeds that have been planted during the small group. Without that water, the seed will fall on the rocky soil, the sun will scorch it, and it will shrivel up and die, "since it had no root" (Mark 4:6).

Encountering Christ during the week on our own makes it possible for us to be "rooted in Christ" (cf. Colossians 2:7) and drink deeply of the "living water" (John 4:10) that he longs to pour into our souls.

Please review the "Encountering Christ This Week" section together as a group during each meeting. This will show everyone that it is an important part of the small group. Ask for feedback each week about how these prayer and reflection exercises are going. However, don't spend too much time on this topic, especially in the early weeks as members become comfortable together and more accustomed to praying on their own.

Asking about their experience with the recommended prayer or spiritual exercise will help you know who is hungry for spiritual growth and who might need more encouragement. The witness of participant's stories from their times of prayer can ignite the interest of others who are less motivated to pray.

About The Evangelical Catholic

The Evangelical Catholic (EC) equips Catholic ministries for evangelization by inspiring, training, and supporting local leaders to launch dynamic outreach. Through training events, services, and ongoing contractual relationships, the EC forms and trains Catholic pastoral staff and lay leaders for long-term evangelical efforts that can be locally sustained without ongoing site visits and regular consulting.

To accomplish this mission, we equip the lay faithful to invite the lost into the joy of life in Christ and stem the tide of Catholics leaving the Church. We form pastoral staff to make disciples, shepherd evangelistic ministries, and manage pastoral structure to make discipleship to Jesus the natural outcome within the parish or university campus ministry.

Our prayer is that through the grace of the Holy Spirit, we can help make the Church's mission of evangelization accessible, natural, and fruitful for every Catholic, and that many lives will be healed and transformed by knowing Jesus within the Church.